# BREAKING MENTAL CHAINS

## Unlocking The 7 Mind Hacks

By: Qaadir'Naqib Muhammad

*Breaking Mental Chains:*
*Unlocking The 7 Mind Hacks*



Printed in the United States of America

Author: Qaadir'Naqib Muhammad

ISBN: 979-8-9903974-4-6

First Printing: 2022
Second Printing: 2024



Published by: Ahvision Publishing
Edited and Book Cover Design
www.AhvisionPublishing.com

# Dedication

I wrote this book in honor of my son, Saadq Muhammad. He is one of the most talented people I know. He is also one of the kindest people that I know. I love you, Saadq Muhammad, and I will that you conquer your fears and embrace your purpose, son.

# BREAKING MENTAL CHAINS

## UNLOCKING THE 7 MIND HACKS

# TABLE OF CONTENTS

# FOREWORD

Finding success, purpose, meaning, and all the things we are innately programmed to strive for looks different for everyone. These goals can be elusive, discouraging, and seemingly out of reach. We, from individuals to global institutions, at times even give up on the idealism of those goals. Why would we do that? Why would we forfeit the birthright of our purpose? For some of us, intentionally systemized barriers have been implemented and nurtured for decades, if not centuries, to ensure the adherence to the intentions of masterful puppeteers who only win when others lose. This is a scarce mindset that the success of the few is contingent on the failure of the many. The direct barriers include redlining, glass ceilings, over-policing, or higher interest rates. But arguably, the indirect barriers cause the most damage and pull us further and further away from our purpose. This book addresses seven of the most notorious and damaging internalized barriers, causing us to be OUR OWN obstacles.

*Breaking Mental Chains: Unlocking the 7 Mind Hacks* is a document that feels as though it was handwritten in isolation by a person obsessed with the forward progression of humankind in the face of unrelenting oppression. Qaadir'Naqib Muhammad took the 26 letters of the alphabet and infused passion, insight, life experience, and dedication into a manuscript that can change someone's life. The great thing about changing one life is that a second life can change, then a third, then a community, then a country, and eventually the world. I look forward to the testimonies of the growth and development of those who decided to read this book with the full intention of becoming their best selves.

We live among a barrage of artificial lives, fragmented experiences, fraudulent successes, misplaced cyber activism, and hollow relationships that contribute to society's lack of autonomy, focus, self-determination, resiliency, and critical thought. This book is a much-needed catalyst for internal change. If the adage, "change oneself, change the world," is true, this book will prompt a change I am eager to see. If not for me, for my children and their children. Brother Qaadir'Naqib has provided two things we need most right now: clarity and instruction. Enjoy your journey, which starts the moment you take action and implement the contents of *Breaking Mental Chains: Unlocking the 7 Mind Hacks.*

***Succeed anyway,***
***Harold G. Branch III***
***Branching Out Coaching and Training Services***
***HomeBase Poetry***

www.TheWellnessPreacher.com
IG: @thewellnesspreacher

# INTRODUCTION

Thank you for getting this book. After realizing that we all suffer from similar thoughts that harm our growth and development as individuals, I decided to look into the cause of these thoughts. I discovered that seven artificial chains play a key role in how we see ourselves and function. In this book, we have laid out a few starting assignments to free you from these mental chains that are preventing you from being the best version of yourself. This is not a lengthy book to go through; it's a concise and information-packed guide designed to enhance your thinking and free your mind. These steps are just some tools for you to start with. These tactics are only the beginning of becoming a free thinker and doer. May you unlock all seven in due time and start to become a free-thinking person as soon as possible.

After each CHAIN, you will see an "***Assignment Page***." This page allows you to complete the assignment you'll receive at the end of those CHAINs. May your journey of Unlocking these **Mental Chains** be successful, enlightening, and, most importantly, fun and exciting.

# CHAIN 1

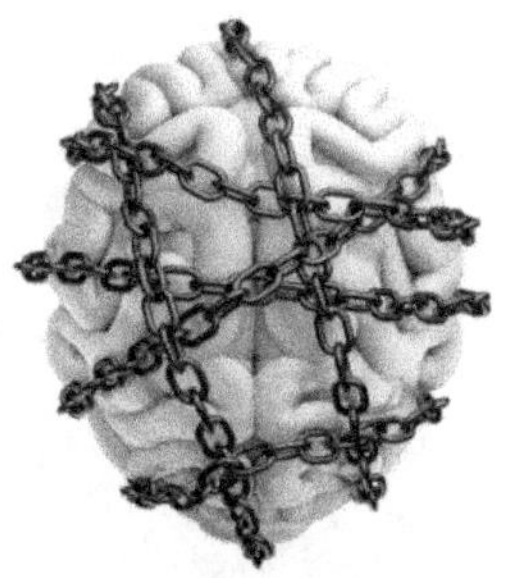

## Entitlement

*"None of us are here of ourselves. All of us were made by others who helped us to become who and what we are. So for us to get the big head, it's an insult to those who helped to make us."*

**The Honorable Minister Louis Farrakhan**

# CHAIN 1
## Entitlement

*The First **Mental Chain** that must be broken is the chain of "Entitlement to do Nothing for Success."*

We must understand that to achieve any measure of success in our lives; we must take charge of our posts. This means that we have to accept the responsibility of self-educating ourselves in the required field that fits our agenda. Depending on your situation, you may have to wear multiple hats at the beginning of your journey to get your ideas off the ground and into a profitable status. This is why educating ourselves is essential.

Let's think about it for those of us who have thoughts that we refuse to share out of fear of judgment and those who want to create a business yet refuse to seek out the information to do so. How many times are you going to sit back and watch other people catch on to an idea you had only the Lord knows how long ago? What's the worst that can happen to you or me when we decide to go after our goals? Is it wrong for you or me to be seen as fearless and bold enough to chase our dreams?

As long as we hide our true thoughts, gifts, and talents from the world, we are dimming our own flame. As long as we place our destiny in the hands of another person, we are decreasing our chances of fulfilling our purpose and increasing our chances of repeating various cycles in our lives. You are worthy, and you deserve the best that life has to offer you. There is no DNA requirement to self-improve our conditions, nor is there a DNA blood type that we must have to enjoy the planet's richness.

You deserve to travel and see the land. It's yours, a gift from the creator so that we can produce whatever we need to sustain ourselves. Unlocking this first mental chain is the only requirement to improve our lives because once we unlock this artificial mental barrier, we are entering into the reality that we are in charge of our lives. Everything from our spirituality, mentality, physical, financial, peace of mind, and overall wellness is all under our control.

Create new thinking patterns and accept the responsibility of determining how successful you are and the type of lifestyle you live. These are major keys to growing forward and unlocking the chain of *entitlement to do nothing for success.* It doesn't matter how long we have been chained to this way of thinking. Whether you are a high school student or a great-great-grandparent, once you become aware of this mental chain, the only question is, are you willing to do the work to break this chain? This chain prevents us from unleashing our truest selves and holds us back from living our best lives while we are alive. We don't have to wait to go to heaven. We can bring heaven to us in this realm of existence while we live if we are willing to do the work to create a thinking pattern that reinforces creating what you think heaven is for you or what you think success is for you in your life.

Everyone's idea of heaven and success is not the same. However, the results of not unlocking this chain are the same for everyone in bondage to its links. They are sitting back, waiting for someone to hand them the career of their dreams or the car of their dreams. They are not taking responsibility for getting it themselves. Instead, they expect things to just happen for them solely because they are alive in this world.

This mental chain keeps us thinking that one day, someone will come and purchase our dream home or send us on an all-expense-paid trip to wherever we desire, and we have not done anything to manifest it. Do you see how crazy that is? This chain tells us to wait for another person to bless us rather than to go out and bless ourselves and enjoy the process of taking our ideas from a thought to reality.

The process of unlocking this chain starts with being honest with ourselves about being in bondage to this mental chain. From there, we must begin to challenge this mentality's behaviors and move differently. Doing the footwork ourselves to get us closer to our dreams is priceless, and embracing the process of making them a reality has its rewards. We must overstand that we are the foundation of how our lives will turn out and accept full responsibility for our thinking and how we spend our time. God brought us on this earth to be great, and it is not a good look if we use our time here putting others in charge of our destiny.

In the "Parable of the Talents," in Matthew 25:14-30, you'll read about three individuals who were given various talents from their lord before he left on a journey. While the master was away, some of the individuals he gave the talents to used them and increased them while one hid his talent. When the master returned, he was pleased with those who used their talents. However, he was upset with the servant, who decided to do nothing with his gift. This parable gives us a clue about how we should use the gifts and talents that God has placed within us.

Do not allow this mental chain to cause you to hide your talent like the man in the parable and cause God to be upset with you for not letting your light shine on this amazing planet. Rise up and break this mental chain of expecting someone to do for you that you can do for yourself. Our perspective of self is a major tool to break away from this mentality because of our view of self and our understanding of self-determination, what we think we can accomplish. Improving the type of thoughts that we allow into our minds will cause us to create new behaviors.

Instead of thinking that we cannot achieve what our heart desires, we start seeing that we can and deserve to do so. Start now and start doing the things that will free you from this thinking of entitlement to what you want in life. You can start by writing out the things you want to accomplish and then discover the steps it'll take to achieve each goal. The main thing is for us to take charge of our lives, including accepting responsibility for achieving our goals. No one else is responsible for manifesting your thoughts and ideas into reality; it's all on you. So the question is, are you ready to break free from this mentality, and are you willing to do something different?

## ASSIGNMENT PAGE

*CHAIN One: Entitlement*

Your assignment is to think of a few things you would Like To ***Manifest*** and then list them in the top section. In the bottom section, write out your ***Action Plan***. Don't forget to research the "How To" of what you're aiming for so that you can make a sound action plan to achieve your goals.

***Manifest:***

***Action Plan:***

# CHAIN 2

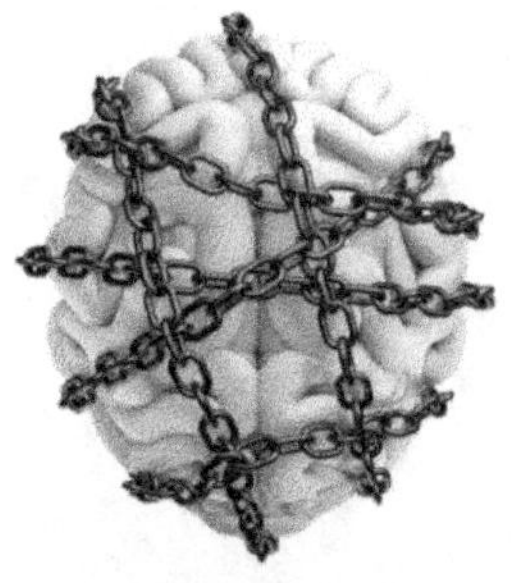

## No Time

*"They say it's not enough hours in a day. It is. Most people just waste the ones we're given."*

**Jvion Jones**

# CHAIN 2
## No Time

*The Second* ***Mental Chain*** *that we must unlock is the chain of "No time."*

Once we realize that we each have been given the same amount of time in a day, we should begin to see that success is not DNA-related. Success is based on how we use our time and nothing more. It doesn't matter what your situation is at this moment. What matters is that you decide whether you want to improve your reality or stay in that same space forever.

Time management is a tool we must learn how to use and a tool we should come to respect because it assists us with staying focused on the task at hand. I remember when I arrived at a meeting with a potential business mentor for myself, and when I walked into his office, he said, "We have three things to discuss, and we have forty-five minutes to do it." The first thing he did was set a timer for fifteen minutes, and each time the timer went off, he repeated the highlights from that conversation and then restarted the timer, and we moved on to the next topic until we reached our time.

This was my first time seeing someone being mindful of their time and aiming to stay on time with their daily tasks. So again, it doesn't matter if you are a single mother or a single father with one or multiple children; it doesn't matter if you have one gig or ten of them. The only thing that matters is deciding how you want to live your life and starting to manage your time.

This mental chain of not having enough time is a lying chain, and at its root, it wants to keep us held back from our fullest potential.

For us to accomplish our goals in life, we will have to organize and prioritize our daily lives so that we can do the things that align with our goals and our daily obligations. Getting up earlier than your usual time to start your day is one way to add time to make your ideas a reality. A sleeping house is a quiet house, and a quiet house is the best time to focus on whatever you need to accomplish, especially if you are writing a book (smile).

A quiet house is also a distraction-free zone and allows you to focus your attention where needed. We have to learn how to set realistic goals with the appropriate time to accomplish them because we can add unneeded stress on ourselves by aiming to complete something in a day that requires a month to do. Learning how to manage our time is the best way to break this mental chain and the best way to start seeing the results that we deserve to see from our efforts. Stop saying you don't have time, and start making time even if you have to stay up late. Get up earlier.

The excitement from working on your ideas and goals will provide you with the energy needed to get through the day. Look at each minute that your eyes are open and ask yourself what you are doing at that moment and if you are not engaging in the activities geared towards achieving your dreams and goals. The first thing you should do is ask yourself, are you serious about getting to the next level in your life? How we spend our time will determine the lifestyle we live because how we manage our time gets us closer to enjoying life the way we deserve to.

As long as we are not taking charge of how our time is managed, we will continue being in bondage with this lying mental chain of not having enough time. God is real, and even he has to manage his time. So if we are the children of the most high God, that makes us Gods too, but with a little "g." If pops have to manage his time so that he can produce his kingdom on earth as it is in heaven, then we, too, as his children, are obligated to manifest our God-given abilities. It's now that we must begin to realize and accept that we have enough time in a day to work on our goals, just like God has enough time to govern all his affairs.

We manage our time enough to get the children to school; we manage our time to get to work and do our jobs; we manage our time to eat; we manage our time to be scrolling on somebody's streaming platform, and we manage our time to do much more with our time. When will we start to navigate our time to become more goal-oriented? When will we begin to focus our minds and time on building our dream lifestyles?

God didn't place you on this earth to be a beggar or just a dreamer. He desires each of us to be doers and great doers, at that. God doesn't do average things and isn't a beggar. God is a DOER. Can you imagine God not being a doer? What are you choosing to be? Take a few minutes out of your day and write out where your time is going. For this to work, you must be honest with yourself about what you do on a day-to-day basis with your time.

At the top, start with the time you usually wake up and then work your way down to when you typically go to bed. Second, review this data and be honest with yourself to realize where you can increase time spent in some places and where you need to decrease time spent in other areas of your life.

You are in control of your destiny, not your parents, friends, or siblings. And none of us can say it's up to God because he gave us free will. Within our free will, God has given us the option to live life less than he wants us to live. Yes, I am saying that God has given us the right to choose freely. We can freely choose to live as doers or as a non-doer. It's our God-given right.

The choice is up to us. The type of thoughts that we have will start to change. But with changed thinking patterns come new behaviors, and unfortunately, this is where many of us veer back to our old ways. Change is a scary place for millions of people, and as soon as they sense change on the horizon, they stop every productive habit they believe is causing this newness. Imagine if we did away with this false mental barrier and started to embrace the newness in our lives. Take time to do a self-assessment and ask yourself how serious you are about living your life to the max because this current thinking and actions are not producing the desired results.

Once we understand how much time we have in a day, it gives us a broader scope of what we can accomplish with proper time management. The more we know, the more we should apply, and we have to learn how to adjust when and where it's needed to generate our ideas from within us to reality. Do you want to remain chained to this link that's holding you back, or will you choose freedom? We have many mental chains that prevent us from enhancing our quality of health and our quality of life overall. This "no time chain" is a master key to the link of mental chains. So, by breaking through this one, we start the process of creating our own thought patterns.

These new thoughts begin to build our confidence. These new thoughts begin to cause a change in how we see ourselves. These new thoughts begin to create more new thoughts, and they begin to cause us to complete more of our goals. We are directly from the creator of the universe. There isn't a thought we cannot manifest, and you have my word. Start taking ownership of your time and stop saying that you don't have enough time in a day to make time to work on accomplishing your heart's desires.

There is enough time in a day to lose weight or to build generational wealth. The question is, are we ready to break through this artificial barrier that has been allowed to be in our minds and start doing the work to manifest our gifts and talents to the world? Today is a great day to start. Don't wait to do the work that'll enhance your life; work on this right away. Start declaring that you will remove the negativity from within and learn how to master time management.

## ASSIGNMENT PAGE

*CHAIN Two: No Time*

Your assignment is to write down what your day-to-day routine looks like as of right now in the bottom section. In the top section, write down what and how you would like your daily routine to be moving forward. Can you SEE yourself living out this routine?

**Day-to-Day Routine Moving Forward**

**Day-to-Day Routine NOW**

# CHAIN 3

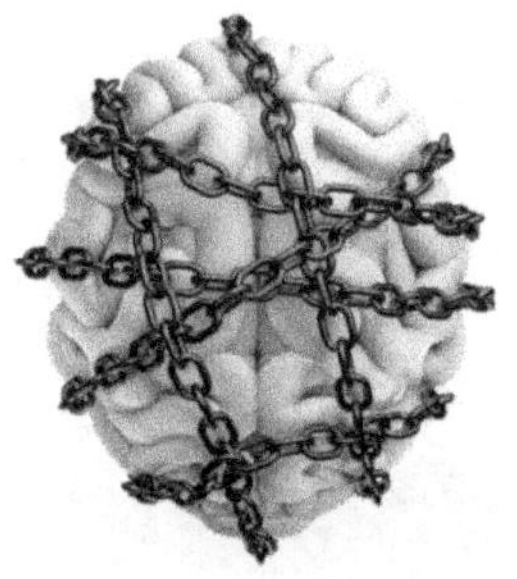

## No Intentions

*"Time must dictate our agenda."*

**The Honorable Minister Louis Farrakhan**

# CHAIN 3
## No Intentions

*The Third **Mental Chain** that must be broken is the chain of "No Intentions."*

This mental chain is just taking life one day at a time rather than operating with the intention of preparing for the future. There are many reasons why this artificial mental chain must be broken. The false fear attached to it prevents us from understanding that we have the ability to impact the world and that future generations can learn from our works. However, this cannot happen if we don't free ourselves from this mental chain that prevents us from living beyond the grave. We empower people through our accomplishments, but if we are not focused on getting anything done, how can others be empowered or inspired by either of us?

We must realize that we all have the option to improve the world for those coming after us for multiple generations to come. If we were to look at the people who have gone before us, we would have to agree that the common denominator between them is that they all lived their lives intentionally, from Nat Turner, Noah, Malcolm X, Muhammad Ali, Tupac, Nipsey, Steve Jobs, Jesus and many more. Each of them lives on because they broke free of this false mental chain of living without intentions.

They used their time here to discover what they were brought on this earth to do. Once they found their purpose for being here, they embraced it and started living intentional lives. The results of how they lived are why we know they have been here on this earth.

Can you imagine if either of these men remained in bondage to this artificial mental chain? What did their choices do for you, and what will your choices do for those coming after you? Are you starting to see the power that you have? Do you see the importance of living life intentionally and how it can be a beacon of light for others in their lives?

## ASSIGNMENT PAGE

*CHAIN Three: No Intentions*

Your assignment is to list at least three people whose lives have inspired you and then write down what they did to inspire you, why it touches you, and what you are doing now because of that person's life touching you.

**1.** ______________________________

______________________________

______________________________

______________________________

______________________________

**2.** ______________________________

______________________________

______________________________

______________________________

______________________________

**3.** ______________________________

______________________________

______________________________

______________________________

______________________________

**4.** ______________________________

______________________________

______________________________

______________________________

# CHAIN 4

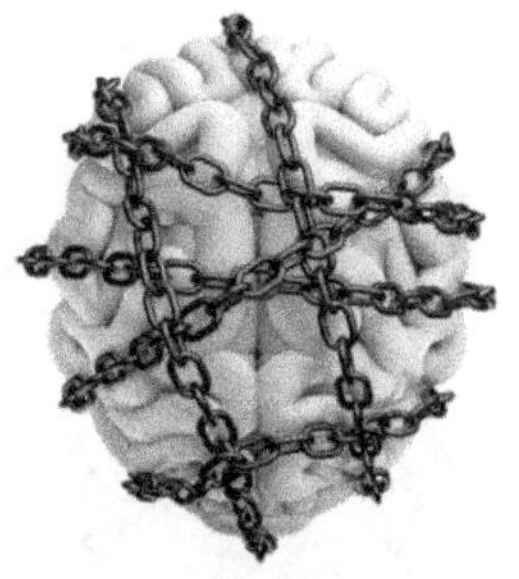

## Irresponsibleness

*"Responsibility finds a way; Irresponsibility makes excuses!"*

**Gene Bedley**

# CHAIN 4
## Irresponsibleness

*The Fourth* ***Mental Chain*** *that we must unlock is the chain of "Irresponsibleness."*

Preparation for the next generation is a must, and being average is unacceptable. This means that we have to accept the responsibility of setting a generational way of living for our family, community, and the generations of our loved ones coming after us. This mental chain is rooted in selfishness and has to be destroyed because it keeps us from seeing how our actions impact our culture as a people.

We can't understand how what we do personally can determine what others do in this mindset. In this chain, we can only understand that we are responsible for self, and self can only affect self. Breaking free from this chain empowers us to see how what we do today can motivate someone tomorrow and understand that this law is not limited to self and our kin. We come from the Earth, so this gives us a direct connection to the planet. This connection to the planet allows us to be responsible for controlling the Earth, and as long as we act according to the laws of the universe, the Earth will enable us to remain in power.

Once we become out of line with the rules and duties of our responsibilities to the earth, it has the right to remove us from its surface. This is done through storms, earthquakes, and other natural disasters worldwide. Whenever we come up short of our responsibilities as children, we have some disasters ourselves with our moms or dads because of our lack of duty to do our chores or not watching after our younger siblings.

We are from the Earth, so we can govern how our planet rotates around the sun and the stars above us. This means that in our lives and the lives of others, we can do our part to dictate how generational behaviors are governed in our friends' and families' lives today.

If the environment that we place our children in is filled with filth and violence, and we add to that environment fear and doubt of going after our goals, what can we expect from our children and the generations to come? If we take our children and place them in an environment that is filled with cleanliness and peace and add to that a space where people love and support you, going after what matters to you, now what would you expect to come out of generations of living and growing up in an environment like this? To envision and understand that this place only exists in this lifetime after we choose to break free of this false mental chain of irresponsibleness is to inspire change in the world. This artificial barrier must be unlocked to understand how our thoughts and actions can make a difference and that our thoughts and actions matter solely because we matter.

We matter to our friends and family, and we matter to the universe. My personal favorite is that we matter to God himself. To break free from this mental chain, we have to start doing things without seeking out how it will benefit us; instead, we must seek how it will impact others. Also, the more we begin to think of how our choices can impact others, we should start to think from a place that includes where others may be in their lives and not solely rooted in what we want and need.

Growing free from this place empowers us to see how we can live beyond the grave because our mission doesn't stop when we are laid to rest. Our assignment can only be fulfilled and completed when human life stops existing. Our post continues on so that those coming after us have a generational behavior code to live by. That code is based on living a purposeful life, removing all excuses to accomplish our goals, and having a high level of humility no matter our accomplishments. We can set this code for ourselves and others if we break free from this artificial chain that keeps us thinking about self and only self.

I once was told that people don't like to take ownership of something because ownership means responsibilities. At the time, I had never been told anything like that before. However, it clicked in my head instantly. At that moment, I realized that those who did not run away from responsibilities were the ones who had that leadership aura attached to them.

We shouldn't fear responsibilities or avoid them due to the accompanying workload of being a responsible individual. The sooner we break free of this mental chain, the better we can grasp our interconnectedness. Our actions today shape our tomorrow. Embracing this truth helps us recognize that we can't simply inhabit God's planet aimlessly. Every creation of God bears a responsibility and a purpose, and yes, that includes YOU.

## ASSIGNMENT PAGE

*CHAIN Four: Irresponsibleness*

Your assignment is to write down ***your purpose*** *and* how you can start being more responsible for the generations coming after you.

---

# CHAIN 5

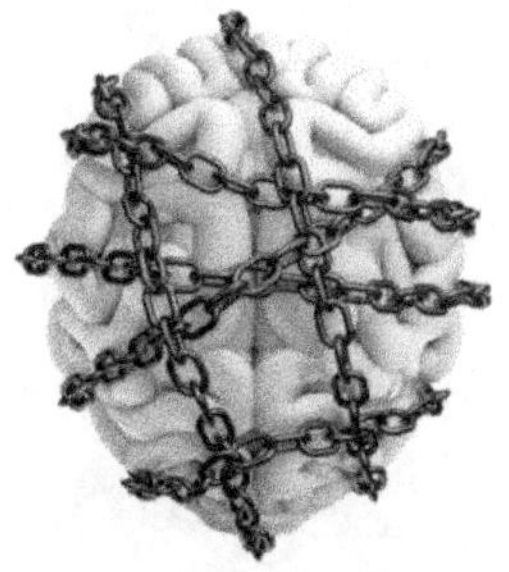

## Ingratitude

---

*"Learn to appreciate what you HAVE before time makes you appreciate what you HAD."*

**Unknown**

# CHAIN 5
## Ingratitude

*The Fifth* ***Mental Chain*** *that must be broken is the chain of "Ingratitude."*

As long as we allow this mental chain to remain, we will always view life from a *woe-is-me* concept, or we will find ourselves never being able to see what we currently possess at this moment in our lives that we can use to improve our condition in life. Those that still hold bondage to this artificial mental chain usually go through life, making statements hinting at how bad things are for them or how nothing ever goes in their favor. Some of us allow this chain to be our primary state of mind, and when this happens, we cannot see anything being in our favor, and everything is working against us.

This state of mind is dangerous because God doesn't like us to be negative thinkers and doesn't want us to be ungrateful for what we currently have. God hates ingratitude, and once we break free from this false mental chain, we will start to see why our higher power dislikes ingratitude. Can you imagine how much work God has to do? Can you imagine doing so much for a person, and then one day you hear them say, "NO ONE HELPS ME," or "I DO EVERYTHING FOR MYSELF." Even better, they talk directly to you in a normal conversation and make such remarks. Do you think that this person appreciates your deeds at that moment, or do you feel that their choice of words will not impact you because you know what you do for them?

As long as we are still connected to this mental chain, we cannot see the things being done in our favor and often miss out on even more blessings because this chain blinds us. This chain causes us to see life from a *what is missing* viewpoint rather than from a *what we have* viewpoint. As long as we overlook what's present in our lives, the opportunities from what we have will be neglected and eventually missed. However, if we decide to move differently, which would be moving in a direction to break free from this mentality that is not adding value to us, It is at that time that we become free from this chain and start to see all the blessings that we have right at our fingertips.

God gives us free will, and we have the ability to enhance our lives and communities, but if we are confined to this state of ingratitude, we will blame God for our situation and do nothing about it. However, after breaking free from this, we begin to appreciate everything in our state of mind. We begin to understand how to connect dots, and we start to bring our ideas into reality, and we start smiling more. Grateful people are always smiling because they can see. They can see that they have everything they need to live the life they desire.

I was having a conversation with someone about someone else, and the person I was speaking to said, "There's something wrong with her; she's always happy." This was so shocking to me that this person saw this individual's ability to be happy all the time as an issue. It was confusing and sad to me because I became aware that we live in a world where others' happiness can threaten others. Ingratitude is the worst state of mind to be in, and it is vital that we break this artificial mental chain that prevents us from seeing properly.

This chain is like a pair of eyeglasses you get—When you put them on, whatever you look at becomes distorted. Once we take the glasses off, we can see things as they are. This is the same for those of us who choose to destroy this false mental chain and break free from it. We will start to see things as they actually are and not a distorted version of the world or our lives.

## ASSIGNMENT PAGE

*CHAIN Five: Ingratitude*

Your assignment is to write five to ten ***things you are grateful for today*** that you once took for granted. If this doesn't apply to you, only write the ten things you are grateful for and never took for granted.

**1.** ______________________________

______________________________

______________________________

______________________________

**2.** ______________________________

______________________________

______________________________

______________________________

**3.** ______________________________

______________________________

______________________________

______________________________

**4.** ______________________________

______________________________

______________________________

______________________________

**5.** ______________________________

______________________________

______________________________

# CHAIN 6

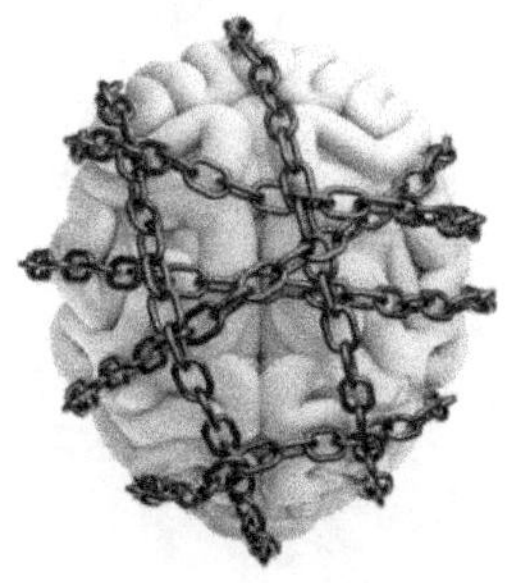

## I Don't Need Anybody

*"If You Want To Go Fast, Go Alone. If You Want To Go Far, Go Together."*

**Ancient Proverbs**

# CHAIN 6

## I Don't Need Anybody

The Six ***Mental Chain*** that must be broken is the chain of *"I don't need anybody."*

This chain is tricky as it can create the illusion that one can succeed without a team or support system. However, once we truly analyze the lives of those functioning within this artificial mental chain, we'll discover that they are doing everything themselves and are running their health and wellness into the ground. They miss out on doing things with their families because they're stuck inside this chain. This chain tells them they are okay and can do it themselves. These false thoughts (artificial chains) are not intended to serve us in our best interest, which is one primary reason we must become free of them immediately.

If we had a team to share the workload, we would have more time for our families. Yes, building a great team that can relate to the mission at hand can be tough. However, it will be worth it once you have linked up with those like-minded and like-hearted individuals who will assist you with getting things done. As long as we think it's okay to do everything ourselves and don't need anyone else, we'll either burn out or run our health and wellness into the ground. This is one reason why many businesses don't last beyond three years. The owners get burned out and lose their desire and inspiration to keep going.

Imagine if they had broken away from this sixth chain and built a team to aid them. How many families could have created generational wealth if those who allowed this chain to overpower them got cleared of this artificial mental chain?

Oprah has a team. Bill Gates has a team, Tyler Perry and Will Smith all have teams, and many other billionaires and millionaires. Many famous people often credit those behind the scenes for their accomplishments. And that is not to say they don't do anything or get any credit themselves. The key is we all need a team. A team doesn't have to be a lot of people. It could be you and two others.

As long as we allow this chain to remain attached inside our minds, it is preventing us from seeing the value of those around us. Unfortunately, this artificial chain often shows potential partners as competitors. This isn't about using people, either. It's solely about aligning ourselves with quality people. We are the best, so we deserve the best of the best in all categories. So, build the best team for yourself and your family.

Once we break free from this mental bondage, we can see what we need and why we need it. For example, if we want to get into flipping cars, we'll need to know multiple mechanics (even if you are one yourself), and we'll also need a network of people. Otherwise, your car business will not last. Look at a used or new car lot, and you will find a service shop, and the size of that dealership will determine how many mechanics they'll have.

To simplify it, we have to go to those who know the information we need or have the skills that will aid us in achieving our desired goal, and if they have both the knowledge and skill, that's even better. If we remain held hostage to this artificial chain, we prevent ourselves from being able to identify what we want out of life so that we can begin to know what our needs are to produce the lifestyle we want.

Our thoughts are powerful, and if we continue to allow negative thoughts to live rent-free inside our minds. We are doing a disservice to ourselves and our friends and family. There will always be individuals and a small group of those who will not understand our vision or intentions. As long as we know those answers, it does not matter what others think about our ideas. However, I want to add that if our intentions are wrong, the results will eventually manifest. So, we should examine our motives before moving out on any thoughts we have. This includes when it comes to building a team for ourselves. The sooner we get free from this chain, the sooner we will start enhancing the reality of our lives and communities.

## ASSIGNMENT PAGE

*CHAIN Six: I Don't Need Anybody*

Your assignment is to generate some ideas and then write down what type of people or services you believe you will need to achieve your required goal.

# CHAIN 7

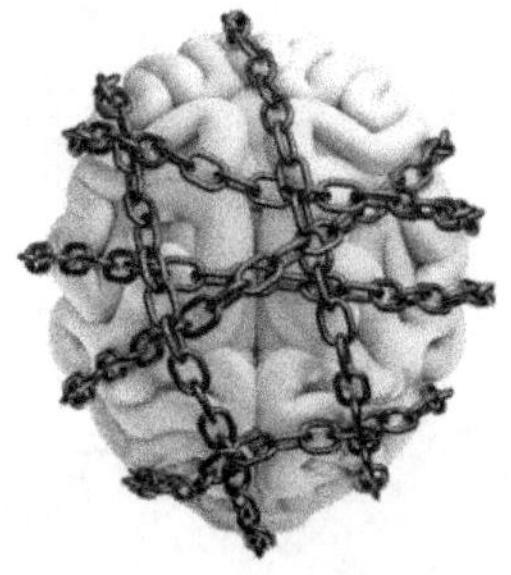

## Everything Comes Before You

*"Only God comes before self."*

**The Wellness Preacher**

# CHAIN 7
## Everything Comes Before You

*The Seven **Mental Chain** that we must unlock is the chain of "Everything Comes Before You."*

This mental chain keeps us in a state of mind that causes us to view everything as important and doable as long as it's not for us. The moment an opportunity comes our way for ourselves, we cannot consider the idea solely because it benefits us. This mentality does not care if you need to improve your health or finances. It will only allow us to see the wants and needs of those around us. This chain has it to where we live life like everything else matters but us when, in reality, we should be living life as if nothing else matters unless we matter.

This is not a selfish state of mind; however, it is more of an "if I am not right, I cannot serve those around me in the best manner" state of mind. We have to break free from this mental chain to start to see the importance of doing things that will reward us, and we have to accept the reality that it is not a bad thing to come first in our lives. Once we are free from this artificial mental barrier, we'll be able to enhance the quality of our lives and the lives of those around us.

Remember that nothing else matters unless you matter; when you are out of whack, everything is out of whack. You deserve to be free from this and live a life of giving and receiving. No one can be happy living under this artificial mental chain. How can we be happy living in a place where we don't matter and everything else does?

Only those held in bondage to this mentality will think that it is possible to find happiness in a space where it is viewed as a sin to take time for yourself. This is often a huge hurdle for mothers to get over as they do their best to focus on providing excellent care for their offspring while avoiding doing anything for themselves.

Mothers, you must break away from this chain ASAP because you are important, and fathers, you're not exempt from this chain. We all must clearly understand how much we matter so that we can start changing our behaviors when it comes to self-care activities. Self-care activities are the things that give us the fuel we need to feel good about ourselves and the fuel we need to face the day-to-day operations of life. While under the influence of this fake chain, we are often running around on an empty tank, sending us to the grave fast.

We are *transmitting beings,* which means we have the capacity to send and receive signals, and when we are only sending out love, time, and resources, eventually, our signal begins to fade and weaken. Let's do our best to transmit properly to continue to grow and enhance our reality. In this state of mind, it's difficult to accomplish our goals because, once again, they benefit us. Often, we can come up with some great ideas but lack the free spirit to lock in the time it will take to achieve those ideas. However, we'll put the same energy and time into the goals and aspirations of others who often suffer from the same false mental chain. Stop pouring time into others and giving your dreams and gifts no time.

Every great "IST" (artist, pianist, dentist, specialist, etc.) had to break free from this chain to master their gifts and talents. It doesn't matter what field we have mastered. The required time to master anything will still be the same: ten thousand hours. Those ten thousand hours are just the master-level entry requirement and not the endpoint of learning for us.

We must break free from this chain before we can start on our ten thousand hours to level up in our field of work. This chain is a hater to our ability to become masters because it only allows us to see the value in others, and it also puts everyone as a priority, and when it comes to us, we just don't matter. If we don't see how wicked this chain is, it's because we have been under its control for too long, and it is time for you to show the world that you matter.

## ASSIGNMENT PAGE

*CHAIN Seven: Everything Comes Before You*

Your assignment for this CHAIN is to write down what you would like to do that will Benefit You And Your Wellness. Then, pick three things that you will make time to do within the next two weeks.

**Top THREE To Make Time For**

**1.**

**2.**

**3.**

# BREAKING MENTAL CHAINS

## UNLOCKING THE 7 MIND HACKS

---

## ABOUT THE AUTHOR

**I am The Wellness Preacher**

Your Brother & Servant

## ABOUT THE WELLNESS PREACHER

The Wellness Preacher, also known as Brother Qaadir'Naqib, was born in Pasadena, CA. At just 37 years of age, he has over twenty years of experience mentoring the generations coming behind him. Growing up in an environment infested with drugs and gang violence, with an absent father and a mother with an addiction, The Wellness Preacher was able to navigate through these circumstances. He avoided becoming a product of his environment and decided to change the narrative of his story.

He is the author of two books and one of the founders of "Fight 4 Life" NO EXCUSES, a (501C3) non-profit organization that teaches life skills to young men between the ages of eight and seventeen. He has earned the name *The Wellness Preacher* from his passion for God, God's word, health and wellness, and his commitment to empowering humanity to do and be better inside and out. Brother Qaadir'Naqib is also a grandfather and father, and he believes that family is business and business is family.

www.TheWellnessPreacher.com
IG: @thewellnesspreacher

# BREAKING MENTAL CHAINS

## UNLOCKING THE 7 MIND HACKS

AHVISION
PUBLISHING

www.ingramcontent.com/pod-product-compliance
Lightning Source LLC
LaVergne TN
LVHW010941110826
845149LV00013B/2700

* 9 7 9 8 9 9 0 3 9 7 4 4 6 *